HE MADE THEIR GLOWING COLOURS

He made their glowing colours

by

VERONICA CHARNLEY

*with colour illustrations
by Martin White
and line illustrations
by the author*

MOWBRAY
LONDON & OXFORD

© Veronica Charnley 1983

ISBN 0 264 66950 9

First published 1983
by A. R. Mowbray & Co. Ltd,
Saint Thomas House, Becket Street,
Oxford, OX1 1SJ

Typeset by Oxford Publishing Services, Oxford.
Printed in Great Britain by The Thetford Press Ltd.,
Thetford, Norfolk.

British Library Cataloguing in Publication Data

Charnley, Veronica
  He made their glowing colours.
  1. Jesus Christ—Biography—Juvenile literature
  I. Title
  232.9'01   BT302

  ISBN 0-264-66950-9

For my Grandchildren
John and Timothy
my
Foster Babies
Foster Children
Playgroup Children too.
Wherever you are,
Whatever you do,
Wherever you go,
May God go, too.

I listen with reverence to the birdsong cascading at dawn from the oasis, for it seems to me there is no better evidence for the existence of God than the bird that sings, though it knows not why. From a spring of untrammelled joy that wells up in its heart.

An Arab Chieftain

CONTENTS

PREFACE

It is said that birds are guided by instinct, independent of reason or experience.

I have, in this story, thrown that idea right out of the window which opens on to the bird table in my garden.

For the past twenty years, one generation of birds after another have come with their families to this table. Not only have the young learned to feed, they have learned to whistle, chirp, call and sing to each other too.

These communicative beings also meet at dawn for their version of Songs of Praise. Whether they ARE singing praises or simply claiming their territory does not matter. The sheer delight, so freely given to those who will listen, compels us to wonder.

Another source of wonder is the sound of the soloist who, sitting on the highest point to be found, sings evensong at sunset. This must be an act of praising God — who else? That Blackbird on top of the tree — how did he get his golden beak? What are the big spots on the breast of the Thrush . . . and how did the little Blue-Tit get his blue cap . . .?

In *He made their glowing colours* I have let the birds tell their own story of the time they spent with Jesus when he lived here on earth.

Veronica Charnley

A messenger comes to Mary

Mary lived with her family and friends in Nazareth, a small town, in Galilee. Every morning she got up very early to say her prayers.

The dawn brought many lovely sounds: a donkey's bray, sheep calling and birds shaking out their feathers — they had no beds to make. Outside Mary's house, a cock crew as he stood on tiptoe, stretching his neck.

While Mary prayed, a little grey pigeon walked up and down, saying,

'Vroo, croo, vroo, croo.'

'How can I say my prayers with you chatting to me all the time?' Mary asked.

'The early bird, you know, you know. He catches the worm, the worm. Vroo, croo. But I don't like worms, just corn, vroo, croo.'

Mary smiled and threw down a few grains of corn, then closed her eyes in prayer. Soon her face warmed as the sun rose higher. Everything was quiet. Too quiet, Mary thought.

Slowly, she opened her eyes. There, in front of her, stood an angel, beautiful, shining, snow-white. He spoke to Mary, saying,

'I am a messenger sent by God. He wants you to be the mother of his baby. His name will be Jesus. One day he will be a king. You must not be afraid of this message or of me.'

Mary WAS a little afraid at the idea of becoming the mother of a king, but she knew that if God asked her to do anything, she must try to do it.

She said,

'Here I am. I will do as God asks.' She closed her eyes.

'Vroo, croo, vroo. I heard the message God sent to you,' called the little pigeon.

When Mary looked up, the angel had gone and the little pigeon was no longer grey, but shining white. He puffed out his chest and showed off his fan-like tail.

'How pretty you are! No longer Pigeon, but Fan-Tail Pigeon,' Mary said, as she put out her hand and warned him, saying, 'Don't be too puffed up as you walk along the top of that wall. You will not see where you are going and you will have a fall. Be careful! You must not be too proud.'

'Vroo, croo,' answered Fan-Tail. Then he sat still to think for a while.

Mary visits her cousin

Mary, so amazed at what had happened, packed up some food and clothing and hurried away to her cousin Elizabeth, who lived with her husband, Zacharias, in the land of Judah.

The hill country was hard and hot, but in the valleys the air was filled with the scent of a number of flowers – roses, lilies, vetch, larkspur and many others.

Mary was not alone on her journey. Many birds sang to her and the flowers looked up to her as she passed by.

When Elizabeth saw Mary coming into the court-yard, she put out her arms to greet her. Elizabeth was going to have a baby, too. She was filled with joy at seeing Mary.

So happy was Mary that she sang a song, called *Magnificat*. While she sang, many birds joined in and the Starlings tried their best to copy her.

'Look at the beautiful colours in their feathers. I wonder how that came about?' asked Elizabeth.

'Down in the valley, the birds flew among all those flowers with their rich colours. They must have collected the colours then, as we came on our way together,' said Mary, pointing into the valley below.

After a lovely holiday of three whole months, Mary went back to Nazareth. In a few months time,

Joseph and Mary went to Bethlehem to be enrolled, among hundreds of other people. The journey was a long one and Mary was rather tired because very soon her baby was going to be born. Joseph's donkey was laden with luggage, but there was just enough room for Mary to have a ride.

In the little town of Bethlehem, the streets were crowded. People shouted and pushed each other. Camels grumbled. Sheep, chickens and goats scattered in all directions in the confusion, as everyone tried to find a room for the night.

Joseph called at an inn, but the landlord shut the door, saying,

'No room! No, no room!'

'But Mary, my wife, she is about to have a baby,' Joseph pleaded. The door opened a little way and the landlord said,

'I tell you there is no room in here. If you go round to the back you will find a stable with hay in the cave. You can share the ox's bed.' The door was slammed shut.

Joseph made Mary as comfortable as he could in what little hay there was. He lit his lantern and a fire.

A little white bird on his way to bed noticed the thin ribbon of blue smoke rising out of a hole in the

roof of the cave. He went to investigate. In so doing, he fell headlong through the hole, scattering ashes and smoke everywhere, but he was not hurt. He hopped and jumped and ran round in circles, trying to shake off the sticky smuts. He cried,

'Tschizzik, tschizzik.'

'Never mind,' Mary said. 'Come little Wagtail. You are now so pretty that we will add to your name. We will call you Pied Wagtail.'

So happy was this little bird that he hopped and skipped and he goes on doing just that, even today.

MAGNIFICAT

My soul doth magnify the Lord:
And my spirit hath rejoiced in God my Saviour.
For he hath regarded:
The lowliness of his hand-maiden.
For behold, from henceforth:
All generations shall call me blessed.
For he that is mighty hath magnified me:
And holy is his Name.
And his mercy is on them that fear him:
Throughout all generations.
He hath showed strength with his arm:
He hath scattered the proud in the imagination of
their hearts.
He hath put down the mighty from their seat:
He hath exalted the humble and meek.
He hath filled the hungry with good things:
And the rich he hath sent empty away.
He remembering his mercy hath holpen his servant
Israel:
As he promised to our forefathers, Abraham and his
seed, for ever.

Jesus is born in Bethlehem

A little brown bird flew into the cave and settled down by the donkey.

'What's going on?' he asked.

'Don't ask me!' said the donkey, who'd been trying to see everything from behind the big, floppy bulk of Ox. Then the donkey said to Ox,

'Do move over. I cannot see what is going on while you are spread all over the place.'

Ox grunted. He was watching, too. They had seen Joseph putting long strips of white cloth out on the hay.

Soon, Mary took one of the pieces of cloth. The animals and birds could scarcely believe their eyes as she wrapped the swaddling bands round a tiny baby.

'What a place to have a baby!' said the little brown bird. He stamped his feet, jumped up and down, then flew right into the inn. The landlord's eyes came out on stalks and his mouth dropped open when the little brown bird burst into song with these words:

> *'Your manger's bare and cold*
> *With little hay and husks of corn.*
> *So, let me help, I'm very bold.*
> *The family there are so forlorn,*
> *That's why I've come to you, next door.*
> *I've come to gather warmth, please, sire.*

Mary and her babe are very, very poor.
I'd like to carry warmth to them,
Gathered from your fire.'

'Warmth?' sniffed the landlord.

The Robin said, 'Quick, quick,'
Then flew away to Jesus
And snuggled at his feet.
Since then, he's worn a waistcoat red.
'I'm glad that I could help,' he said.

The shepherds in the fields saw a great light. One said that he could hear a lark.

'A lark? In the middle of the night?' The other shepherds laughed. Then, one by one, they ALL thought they heard the lark. It seemed to sing,

'Quick, quick, now hark.
Hear the angels sing.
Follow me; it is not dark.
Come and see the King.'

Snow was falling gently as the shepherds made their way down the hill. Not far from the cave, they met a Blackbird. They thought it very strange, meeting a Blackbird in the middle of the night. He had a beak of bright gold, the brightest they'd ever seen. The shepherds asked,

'Beautiful Blackbird, alert and sleek,
How did you get your golden beak?'

'Inside the cave, the night became day
As I looked on a baby, asleep in the hay.
Through a hole in the roof, the snow fell
and dripped
And I noticed the baby's halo had slipped!
Stuffing the hole in the roof with a feather,
I shielded the baby against the bad weather.
Then, moving the halo from where it had rolled,
I put it back, like a crown of gold.
Thank you for calling me beautiful, sleek.
That's how I got my golden beak.'

The shepherds moved quietly into the cave and knelt down before the baby, who was wrapped in swaddling bands and lying in the manger. One of the shepherds gave Jesus a lamb. The others watched with wonder.

All at once, there was a terrible noise outside the cave. The shepherds had gone back to their sheep in the hills and it was morning. Birds were whistling, chirping and chatting at the tops of their voices.

'Oo, oo, oo. Whatever is the matter?' asked Little Owl, as he passed by.

'We're trying to find the bird with the best carrying voice. One who will spread the good news about the new-born King all over the world!' they chanted.

'I only hoot,' said Little Owl, looking down his short, fat beak.

'We're not asking you,' said a bossy, busy Great

Tit.

'Oo, oo, oo,' called Little Owl, as all the little birds began to mob him.

Suddenly, all was quiet. Every bird sat still and listened. Someone called. It was a long, shrill, trilling call, which turned into song.

'I am a little, brown bird,
Darting here and there,
My tail a tiny periscope,
My song a loud, shrill air.
I'm heard in heaven and on earth.
I'LL proclaim the baby's birth.
You cannot guess? I'll tell you then.
My name is little Jenny Wren.'

It was with joy that all the other birds sent Jenny Wren on her way to spread the good news.

Two Long-Tailed Tits sat on a branch to discuss what birthday gift they could give to the baby.

'We've nothing pretty, only black, grey and white feathers,' sighed the first.

'That's it, then. Feathers,' said the second.

'We can't give FEATHERS!' said the first.

'It's feathers or nothing,' answered the second. The first Long-Tailed Tit drew back from the second, saying,

'I'm not pulling out feathers! It hurts!'

'I'll do it for you. Now, close your eyes and take a deep breath. Ready?'

'Ouch! Steady on! That's enough. Stop!'

After much squeaking and feather-pulling, the little birds flew to the manger and dropped their feathers into the tiny, pink, outstretched hand of Jesus.

'What a lovely, warm present you have brought for the baby! But I do believe you are blushing,' Mary said, smiling. 'Or have you brushed the winter sky?' she asked.

> *'No. We came to Bethlehem to think,*
> *What* CAN *we give to Jesus?*
> *Our feathers, now, have added pink,*
> *But not without a fuss!*
> *So now, we hope we'll make folk think*
> *— and ask*
> *How* DID *those feathers turn to pink?'*

Happy, the Long-Tailed Tits flew on their way.

'Si, si, si,' said one to the other when they met a large bird with a long tail. He was very black and his beak was full of bright gifts. The Long-Tailed Tits asked,

'Are those gifts for Jesus? It's his birthday, you know.'

'Yes, I do know. Jenny Wren told me. No, they are not for Jesus. I don't give gifts, I collect them. I am a Magpie, a collector of things. When I've dumped this lot at home, I'm off to Bethlehem for gold.'

'Gold?'

'That's right. Haven't you seen Blackbird since he's been to Bethlehem? He's collected enough gold to cover the whole of his beak! That new-born King, he's got gold. I'm off.'

Magpie, iridescent as a rainbow in the sunlight, flew away, chuckling to himself.

'Si, si, si, he's very greedy,' squeaked the little birds as they wiped their beaks on a branch, as if to wipe out all ugly thoughts about Magpie.

A few days later, when Magpie returned from Bethlehem, all the other birds flocked together. They whispered. Some peeped through their feathers; others looked over their wings. The sight of Magpie in all those bandages scared the birds.

'Whatever has he done?' they asked.

'He's been up to no good.'

'He's been stoned!'

'Maybe he's been shot with an ARROW.'

All sorts of ideas filled the minds of these birds. Not one of them would go up to Magpie and ask what had gone wrong, so they formed a group and sang to him.

> *'Magpie, magpie, collector of things*
> *Bright as the colours within your wings,*
> *Why are you wrapped in bandages white?*
> *Are you wounded? Did you fight?'*

'No, I just wanted the golden light
Surrounding the baby that cold winter night.
But Mary, who stroked me, explained, then said,
"Have some of his swaddling bands instead."
That's how I got these bands of white.
Now I must help to spread the light
Christ came to bring, that cold winter night.'

Back in the cave, Mary laughed as she watched a little Tom Tit. He was a great gymnast, with all his twisting and swinging upside down.

'You will get very hot doing all those tricks. Your pretty green and yellow feathers will not keep you warm enough when you go outside. I will make a coat and cap for you from the hem of my blue cloak,' she said.

'That sounds fun,' chirped little Tom Tit, as he flew to swing on the manger.

Mary got busy with pine needle and cobweb thread. Every stitch was a prayer. A prayer for all the little birds and the big ones, too. A prayer for her baby, the ox, the donkey, Joseph and the angel who'd brought her that message. The donkey watched as the needle went in, out, in, out. He did not like missing things. Soon the clothes were ready and Mary called Tom Tit to her side.

Joseph was standing at the entrance to the cave. He watched as Little Owl swooped down and rested on a shed.

Mary called Joseph to look at Tom Tit in his new coat and cap. Joseph smiled, then sang softly,

'A little Tom Tit by the manger bare
Watched over the new-born King.
An ox, an ass and Mary were there,
They heard the angels sing.
Mary was dressed in palest blue,
Tom Tit in yellow and green.

"I'll make a coat and cap for you,
The best you've ever seen!"
The ox, the ass and Mary all smiled
When they saw the perfect fit.
Go, little bird, tell every child,
Your name is not Tom, it's little Blue Tit.'

Jesus was fast asleep and Joseph walked outside again. He walked over to the shed, put out his arm and Little Owl walked on to it, looking very sad.

'Why are you so sad? Are you hungry?' Joseph asked.

'Oo, oo, kiew, noo, oo. Not hungry; I am able to hunt by day as well as by night. I feel sad because when I told the birds that I could only hoot and not sing, they mobbed me. I want to see the baby. Is this where he is? Jenny Wren told me about him. I watched that big star over there.'

'That's right. I saw you arrive. Let me show you the baby, then I will sing YOU a song.'

Joseph and Little Owl looked into the manger. Then Joseph stepped back and sang,

> *'Dear Little Owl, the smallest, so wise,*
> *With rings of light around your eyes,*
> *Staring, you watched till the star was still*
> *Across the valley, by a cave in the hill.*
> *Swooping, you stayed on a nearby shed.*
> *Who do you see in the manger bed?'*

> *'Kiew, guess who lies in the hay?*
> *Kiew, 'tis Jesus born today.'*

> *'His halo we see in your eyes reflected,*
> *His wisdom, too, in you perfected.*
> *Dear Little Owl, the smallest, so wise,*
> *'Tis HIS light we see around your eyes.'*

As Joseph stroked the head of Little Owl, he said,

'Now you can carry Christ's light wherever you go.'

Little Owl flew away into the night. As he went, Joseph called,

'Goodbye, Little Owl, goodbye.'

'Kiew, kiew, oo, oo,' the Owl called back.

Jesus is presented at the Temple

In the morning, Joseph fed and watered the donkey. He prepared him for the few miles walk to Jerusalem. Every baby boy had to be taken to the Temple to be presented to the Lord. Mary and Joseph, like everyone else, had to take with them a pair of Turtle Doves or two small Pigeons for a sacrifice, an offering. Joseph and Mary chose to take a pair of Turtle Doves.

'They are such gentle birds,' Joseph said to Mary.

'Yes,' said Mary.

'When we hear them, we know that winter is past. Solomon sang about them, didn't he?'

'That's right. He loved their soft voices,' said Joseph.

'Croo, oo, oo. Who was Solomon?' asked one of the Doves.

'Why, he was King of Israel and he sang a lovely song about you and me. Well — partly about our family,' said the other Dove. Then he asked,

'Shall I sing some of his song to you?'

'Go on, then.'

The Dove took a deep breath. At the same time, the feathers on his chest all puffed out and a beautiful sound came from between his beaks. This is what he sang.

'Rise up, my love, my fair one and come away.
For lo, the winter is past, the rain is over and gone.

The flowers appear upon earth.
The time of the singing of birds is come
And the voice of the Turtle is heard in the land.'

The Doves cooed to each other as they were carried in their basket to the Temple.

When the Holy Family arrived, the donkey stood outside the Temple, motionless, his head bowed. He was saying a prayer for the Turtle Doves, who had looked at him through their basket as Joseph carried them inside.

In the Temple stood a very old man. His name was Simeon. He knew that he would not live for very much longer and he had one great wish. He wanted to see Jesus. So Simeon went to the Temple each day, knowing that before long Jesus would be brought there.

As Simeon stood, he prayed that he might see the Light of the world, Jesus, before he died. He turned round and there, on the steps of the Temple, was Mary. She held Jesus up to the old man who took him in his arms and blessed God. Then he sang a song called Nunc Dimittis and the Holy Family returned to Bethlehem.

Old Simeon went to his own home. He was a very happy old man.

NUNC DIMITTIS

Lord, now lettest thou thy servant depart in peace:
According to thy word.
For mine eyes have seen:
Thy salvation,
Which thou hast prepared:
Before the face of all people;
To be a light to lighten the Gentiles:
And to be the glory of thy people Israel.

The three Kings bring their gifts

The Holy Family stayed on in Bethlehem and Jesus was visited by the people of the town.

One morning, a strange noise woke Mary earlier than usual. She heard a scratching, a sweeping sound on the floor of the cave. It was too dark to see anything.

'Joseph, Joseph! Wake up!' she whispered. Joseph didn't move.

'Joseph, wake up! What is that sweeping sound?' Mary shook Joseph's shoulder and he sat up. Mary put her finger to her lips and whispered again.

'Listen.'

'Who's there? What do you want?' Joseph asked. There was no answer, so he lit his lantern and held it high up. There was the answer. A Peacock was using his long black and blue tail like a broom. Joseph stood up. His lantern cast strange shadows on the walls of the cave. For a moment, Peacock stood straight up without moving. He looked all round the cave.

'You need not sweep up for us,' said Joseph. 'We will do it later, by daylight.'

'That will be too late, much too late. I am preparing for my masters, the three Kings from the east. You will hear me announce their arrival.'

Peacock screeched so loudly that Jesus woke up and cried.

'I'm sure we shall hear you,' Joseph said, picking Jesus up. Peacock jerked his head backwards and forwards, as he strutted out of the cave. He flew to the top of a wall and there he kept watch.

After all the noise, Mary washed and changed Jesus. Then she fed him and afterwards, she let him play in the hay.

Mary and Joseph finished their breakfast and went outside. The sun was creeping into the sky in the east. They watched and wondered why there was such a cloud of dust in the distance. Peacock stood up on the top of the wall and screeched. Mary ran back into the cave so that Jesus would not be too frightened by the noise.

From the clouds of dust came flocks of little birds. They all sang and flew up and down with excitement. Joseph looked closer. He heard voices. As men poked with their sticks, the camels grumbled. Peacock jumped from the wall and walked with slow steps towards the men and awaited his orders.

Joseph went into the cave and settled Mary in the hay, with Jesus on her lap. Then the great noise came. Peacock screeched and stood just inside the cave. The whole place was filled with bright sunlight. Peacock stood to one side and opened out that long black and blue tail of his into a magnificent, giant fan, studded with jewels of every colour, black, green, red, blue, gold and rich brown. Not real jewels, of course, but the most wonderful feathers any other bird had ever seen.

When Peacock made the announcement of the arrival of the Kings, Jesus hid his face in the folds of his mother's cloak. The donkey's ears fell back on to his neck and he closed his eyes. Then, all was silent.

The donkey opened his eyes again and watched.

The three Kings glided into the cave.

'The star guided us,' they said and fell down and worshipped Jesus.

Opening their gifts, they offered him gold, frankincense and myrrh. They spoke in turn, saying,

'My gold is a token of your kingship.'

'My frankincense will lift up our prayer.'

'And my myrrh signifies the pain and suffering to come.'

The Kings spoke gently and Jesus turned from the shelter of Mary's cloak and reached out to them. There was a moment of silence and a great stillness. Even the donkey kept his ears from twitching. Soon the three Kings left. They went out, crossing the hills and valleys into their own homes.

The birds had been silenced, too, by the peaceful scene in the cave that day, but, one by one, as the sun began to go down, more and more birds began to tune up for evensong. In front of all the other birds stood the Mistle Thrushes. They carried the music on their waistcoats. The big black notes were easy for the birds to follow as they sang. The Song Thrushes, who sing all the year round, sounded the tuning note, because they had perfect pitch.

Choral evensong was sung on the night that the Kings left, in celebration of the visit. The angels who'd sung on Jesus' birthday joined in the singing with the birds.

'Hear us sing, glory to the new-born King.'

The journey by night into Egypt

After evensong, the birds found places to rest and sleep. The sun had gone to bed, but a few stars came out to look at the night sky.

A beautiful Barn Owl was out and about. He glided silently, listening for sounds which told him that food was near. It did not matter that he could not see in the pitch darkness, because God had given him the gift of perfect hearing. If a mouse squeaked, if a frog croaked or if a moth landed on a leaf within the hearing of Barn Owl, not only were their days numbered, but their last seconds, too. All these and other little creatures made tasty meals for Barn Owl.

During the night following the wonderful choral evensong, Barn Owl was silently hunting when he heard a flute-like call; a sad, pleading call.

'Pioo, pioo,' came the notes, softly at first, then becoming louder and louder.

'PIOO.'

'Whatever is the matter?' asked Barn Owl, as he glided on to a branch close to an unhappy Nightingale.

'Joseph! It's Joseph! He cannot sleep. He has had a bad dream and he doesn't want to wake Mary or Jesus. But he must! He is in great danger!'

'Nonsense,' said Barn Owl. 'Not after all the joy of yesterday.'

'There is danger, I tell you,' wailed poor Nightingale. 'Herod, that wicked king, told the three Kings to go back and tell him where Jesus had been born, but they have gone home another way without calling on Herod. They were warned not to tell him, during the night, so they didn't see Herod again and now Herod has lost his temper and. . . .'

'Kings don't lose their tempers, do they?' interrupted Barn Owl.

'King Herod has. He is so jealous because Jesus is a King that he has sent soldiers out, armed with swords. They are not to go home again until they have found Jesus and KILLED him.'

It did not matter how bitterly Nightingale cried. Barn Owl said, calmly,

'Being jealous won't help one little bit. Herod will make himself ill.'

'Oh, do hurry! An angel has told Joseph that he has got to get away fast; as fast as he can, with Mary and Jesus. He has to go while it is still dark.'

'Go where?'

'To Egypt.'

'Why Egypt of all places? I don't see what I can do. Anyway, I haven't had enough supper to keep me going on a journey.'

'Really, Barn Owl, you must stop thinking of yourself all the time. Pioo, pioo. In the light of Joseph's lantern, you will look as white as snow. Even your beautiful golden buff coat will look as white as your underclothes and with your perfect hearing, you will know of any danger on the way, long before Joseph does. Come on, Barn Owl!'

Barn Owl gave a long sigh. He rather enjoyed those kind words from Nightingale.

'Very well. You'd better wake Mary and Jesus. Go and sing them a song, while I speak to Joseph.'

The two birds flew to the cave. Barn Owl seemed to float inside, while Nightingale sat outside and sang a gentle song. Her flowing, almost liquid notes reached Mary, who sat up to listen.

> *Wake, wake up and hear.*
> *The night is dark and danger's near.*
> *Come, come, come away*
> *Fast, before the break of day.*
> *Barn Owl here will show you where.*
> *He'll guide your path, he'll get you there.'*

Mary held Jesus close to her, wrapping him up against the cold night air.

The donkey stumbled to his feet. He hated being disturbed in the night, but he never said anything. Like so many donkeys, he was quiet and very patient. He carried Mary and Jesus, while Joseph led him along the path where Barn Owl flew, lit by the light of Joseph's lantern.

After some time they found themselves in Egypt, their place of safety.

'Thank you, dear Barn Owl, for your help along the way,' said Joseph, as Barn Owl flew off in search of food once more.

Nightingale felt she had to stay close by the Holy Family. They were very tired and as the sun had not yet risen, there was still time for them to get some sleep before the beginning of a new day. So Nightingale sang a short lullaby.

> 'Hweet, hweet,
> Dear family, sleep.
> Rest your heads, your hands, your feet.
> Hweet, hweet,
> Be still, be calm, just sleep'.

Back in Bethlehem the next morning, the birds found the cave empty. They were so sad, so puzzled, that they sang no dawn chorus. The sky was sad, all dressed in grey. When the landlord of the inn went to take his Ox to work, the poor animal took long, slow, sad steps along the way.

'Croo, croo, oo,' cried a little Dove. 'Our baby King has been taken away.' All the birds began to sob. All except one.

Now, Nightingale, who sings by day as well as by night, sat high on a rock and filled the air with mellow tunes.

'Voo, croo, how CAN you sing when our King has left us and we don't know where he has been taken?' asked the Dove.

'But I DO know where he is! I went with them all and now I am back to tell you about the journey we had to make in a hurry. We had to go all the way to

Egypt and now I've flown the whole way back without a stop. Where are all the Wrens? We must find them and tell them to spread the news. We must all try to follow Jesus.'

As Nightingale spoke, a soft breeze carried her questioning notes to where the Wrens had all spent the night, huddled together for warmth.

'Hist, hist,' squeaked the sleepy Wrens. 'We are being called.' One by one, they left their dormitory. Darting from crevice to crevice in the walls and under the stones, they helped themselves to tasty, half-awake insects who were too sleepy to run away.

'Ooze, oo,' said a baby earth-worm, slipping backwards into his hole. 'That was a close one! I nearly got swallowed up that time.' He flopped back into his mother's slippery lap and collapsed. She said,

'How many times have I told you not to go digging so near the surface early in the morning? Many times I've told you that the early bird CATCHES the worm. You have nearly lost your head once and now you have lost the end of your tail! What are you going to do about that, I'd like to know?' Mother worm went on and on like many mothers, but it was only because she loved her baby worm so much. She was always thinking about him, hoping that he was safe.

'Are you listening to me?' she asked, turning bright pink. 'What will you do if you lose ALL your bottom half and not only the tip of your tail?'

'Grow it again,' smiled baby worm, sliding his long, thin face against his mother's, with a slippery kiss.

'Oh, be off with you! Get stretched! Don't go down too far, the moles might eat you,' she called, teasing.

'There's no safety in this earth,' sighed baby worm, as he slithered away.

When all the Wrens had met near Nightingale,

with all the other birds, they listened to the story of
the flight into Egypt and how Barn Owl had led the
Holy Family.

Nightingale said,

'Go often to see Jesus; he loves to throw some
crumbs out for you. He watches the birds, then
laughs and claps his hands with delight when they
get really close. He will not be trying to frighten
you, he will love to see you. Sometimes, Mary says to
him — "No, Jesus, not all for the birds.
You are meant to be eating that bread." When Jesus
tries to walk,' continued Nightingale, 'sometimes he
falls and bumps himself. Then Mary picks him up,
cuddles him and says — "Sh, what's that? Listen to
the birds" — and then Jesus forgets that he has had
a bump.'

One night, after Jesus had been put to bed, Joseph
and Mary stood talking in the twilight, when they
heard a distant, rumbling. The sky looked angry.

'Surely, there will be a storm tonight. We had
better go inside,' said Joseph.

Not only was it stormy outside that night.
Joseph's mind was stormy, too. He kept tossing and
turning until something woke him. He had been
dreaming, but he could not remember what it was
about. He got up and went to stand at the door. He
wanted to clear his mind. He was amazed to see
Nightingale sitting there. She did not sing. She
knew what was happening and waited to see what
Joseph would do.

As Joseph stared out into the night, his dream
came back to him. Yes, another angel had come to
him and said,

'You must get up and leave. Take Mary and Jesus
with you. The wicked King Herod is dead, but his
son has come to the throne and he is no better than
his father. He, too, will want to kill Jesus. You will

have to go NOW, tonight.' And the angel left him.

Nightingale watched Joseph lower his head into his hands. She flew to his side, whispering,

'Do not distress yourself, Joseph. I will contact Barn Owl. We will guide you to a safer place.'

Joseph knew that Nightingale would keep her word. He watched her fly into the darkness. He did not want to wake Mary and Jesus until he had to do so. As he waited for Nightingale, the time seemed to go so slowly. Then, at last, he heard a flutter.

'I just cannot wake Barn Owl. He only says — "lovely supper, juicy meal." I think he is dreaming. But don't worry, I have a plan.'

Joseph listened to Nightingale.

'I have been in contact with our sister, Moon. She says she will be wearing her silver frock tonight, which means we shall have light enough for our journey.'

Gently, Joseph said to Mary, as he woke her and told her about the dream,

'Let us return to Nazareth, our home.'

When Nightingale heard that, she hastily scratched a message in the sand. It read,

'Follow me to Nazareth — Nightingale.'

'There,' she said, 'I think the other birds will be able to read that when they wake in the morning.'

Jesus grows up in Nazareth

Joseph and Mary were quick to settle down again in Nazareth.

'I am glad we have come home,' Mary said to Joseph.

Jesus was happy, too. He enjoyed taking a picnic into the hills with his friends. They climbed trees and played in the olive groves and in the caves in the hillside.

One day, Jesus was climbing a tree, when the branch on which he stood broke. There were peals of laughter, but not from Jesus or his friends. They looked around, but could see no one.

'You should never stand on a branch which has no leaves on it, Jesus. A branch without leaves is a dead branch, very dangerous. Have you hurt yourself?'

The children were worried. They heard the laughter again. Suddenly, their fears turned to joy and they laughed, too, as they watched a beautiful green Woodpecker land on the broken branch which had fallen when Jesus was climbing. Woodpecker began to knock the tree, very, very fast.

'See? I am a tree surgeon, a doctor. I clean up all the bad sores on the trees. I keep them well. Not only that, I open up new larders full of good food.' Woodpecker laughed again and flew away.

'We seem to learn something new every day,' said

Jesus to his friends.

'Like us, like us,' sang all the birds. 'We have learned about the little town of Bethlehem where you were born, about the shepherds and Simeon and the Kings and the journeys you had to make by night. Each springtime, all the new baby birds are taught about you.'

The little birds chatted on and on as Jesus and his friends ran down the hill into the valley and up the other side into Nazareth, where they went into their own homes.

When Jesus saw his mother, he asked,

What is happening? Why are you putting clothes and food into a bundle?'

Mary answered,

'We have to go to Jerusalem tomorrow. Had you forgotten?'

'Passover again already? It seems only yesterday that we were there, not a whole year.'

'Well, it is. You had better go to bed early tonight. We are starting early in the morning to avoid the crowds,' Mary said.

There certainly were crowds as the people gathered in Jerusalem for the Feast of the Passover.

The birds, who kept watch over the Holy Family, began to feel worried because they lost sight of Jesus. The donkey, Mary and Joseph walked for a whole day searching for him. Then, they returned to Jerusalem to look again.

All the birds fluttered round the walls and ramparts to the Temple, hoping to catch sight of Jesus.

After three days, as the birds were roosting sorrowfully in and around the Temple, tired after their searchings, suddenly they all took to the air. They'd been frightened by two people rushing into the Temple. When they saw that the two were Joseph and Mary, the birds settled down again and watched.

'There you are, Jesus! Three days we have cried and searched for you! Why did you run off? Why did you not say where you were going?' Mary was very unhappy.

Many of the young birds began to wonder whether THEIR mothers were worrying about THEM. But they were comforted when they watched Jesus and heard him say,

'Mother, look up! Look at all those birds. They are still young, but they are out and about, learning: learning how to fly, to build, to sing. Singing is their work for God. They have left their nests. Don't you understand that I, too, must be about my father's work? I must learn. I must do work for my father in heaven.'

Hearing Jesus speak like that made Mary remember the day when the angel brought a message to her and said that she was to be the mother of God's Son, Jesus. That made Mary realize that she would have to let Jesus grow up. She would have to learn to love him and let him go.

Back in Nazareth, Jesus helped Joseph for some years in the carpenter's shop. Then it seemed no time at all before Jesus was grown up.

Jesus is baptized and tempted

Jesus left home one day and made his way to the River Jordan. There he was baptized by a man called John the Baptist, who poured water on to Jesus' head. At that moment, a breeze passed by. It whispered to the trees,

'Bow your branches! Dip them into the cool waters and listen to the voice from heaven.'

'Voice from heaven?' asked a small group of birds as they tightened their grip on the dipping branches.

'Yes, listen to the message I bring from heaven,' said the gentle breeze.

As Jesus walked from the shallow waters, a light shone round about him and a pure white Dove glided silently over his head. The birds watched and listened, but they didn't understand about repentance. The breeze said that everyone must repent of their sins.

'Oo, oo, oo,' said Little Owl. 'I know what that means. You must say you are sorry when you have been naughty, oo, oo, oo.'

Almost before Little Owl had finished speaking, the breeze began to sound like a song, singing as it went by,

> 'This is the day the Spirit came.
> Jesus will heal and teach and guide.
> He'll wash our greatest sins away.
> For ever with us he will abide.'

The Spirit then led Jesus into the wilderness. Jesus was to have time away from all worldly things. No food, no people, no house where he could sleep, but time alone with the Spirit of God. He was going into retreat.

This made all the birds very lonely. Some were quite upset.

'There are prowling wolves up there,' said one.

'And great big birds of prey, looking for the dead bodies of sheep and goats,' said another.

Some birds flew a little way into the wilderness and stood as high as their thin legs would stretch, hoping to see Jesus in the distance.

'Please Barn Owl, fly out there and see if Jesus is all right,' begged the little birds.

Poor Barn Owl came back looking very sad. He had seen Jesus with stones for his pillow and only earth for his bed. The nights were freezing and the days scorching hot.

Sadly, the birds waited. They wanted Jesus back. But in the wilderness, Jesus had a visitor, a wicked angel called Satan, who came from the dark and terrible underworld. He knew that Jesus was living in the spiritual world only for a while, so Satan tried to upset him.

'You DO look hungry. Why don't you change these stones into bread? Why don't you change that dirty pool of water into wine? Go on!'

Jesus did not answer.

Then Satan said,

'Come up into the mountain with me.' Jesus went. There, on the edge of a steep slope, they looked down over miles and miles of country.

'If you do as I ask, if you follow my ways, all that you see in front of you and lots more, too — it will be all your very own. You must be even more hungry now. Come on, change these stones into bread.'

Jesus looked at Satan and said,

'Man shall not live by bread alone, but by every word that comes from the mouth of God. Get thee behind me, Satan. Leave me alone.'

Jesus worked really hard to do the will of God. He fought Satan off and when good, beautiful angels came to comfort Jesus, Satan went back into the underworld, a crushed enemy.

Jesus heals the sick

After his time in the wilderness, Jesus went back to Nazareth for a while to be with Joseph and Mary. All the birds were happy again and the air was filled with song.

Jesus talked to his mother about the difficult time he had had in the wilderness and told her of the good angels who came to help him fight the enemy, Satan.

'Temptation is very difficult to overcome,' he said.

'For all of us, Jesus,' Mary answered.

Shortly after this, Jesus went to live in a place called Capernaum. There, he taught everyone how to be forgiving, how to love one another and how to live part of every single day for God. He helped the sad, the sick, the lonely and people followed him wherever he went.

'They MOB him,' cried the birds. 'They mob him far more than we ever mobbed Little Owl. We must protect him.'

In the evening, the birds fell asleep as the sun went down, but Jesus stayed awake. He had work to do. But Barn Owl, with his perfect hearing, nudged the birds awake again. Some peeped out from under their feathers. They wondered what the strange shuffling sound was. Then they heard whisperings; there was some crying, too.

'Si, si, si. Whatever is going on?' squeaked the

Long-Tailed Tits. In the half-light, they watched people being carried, people using walking-sticks, some on crutches, others crawling along the ground. The blind were being led by friends, the deaf followed, looking into the twilight, wondering what was going to happen.

As the darkness fell, the birds could keep awake no longer. They slept soundly.

The next morning, they were amazed to see heaps of old walking-sticks, crutches and a pile of dirty, blood-stained bandages lying about. All the people had gone. Then they heard their friend, the handsome cock, crowing and their puzzle was solved. This is what they heard.

> 'Cock-a-doodle-do.
> Now listen, all of you.
> No need to fear,
> The deaf will hear,
> The blind shall see,
> The lame will learn to walk.
> The dumb, they too, shall talk.
> Once more the dead shall live.
> New life he's come to give.
> Give thanks, whenever you
> Hear my cock-a-doodle-do.'

Hearing this, the little birds sang a more lovely dawn chorus than usual. Then, they flew to find Jesus. He was in a place all by himself, thinking things over. He was tired, too, after all the healing he had done the night before.

He called all the birds to him and explained that he needed help.

'I am going to the beach where the fishermen are on the shores of Lake Galilee. Wings up, who would like to come, too?'

Jesus smiled when he saw so many wings pointing

to the sky and the birds were so happy that they
burst into song.

'Oh, happy, happy dawn,
Oh, gentle, misty morn.
We are to help our Lord to find
Some helpers, good and kind.
Men to listen, men to hear,
Men who'll work, discarding fear.'

Jesus chooses his twelve Apostles

Down on the shore, Jesus saw a man in his boat. He called out,

'Andrew, follow me.' Straight away, Andrew left his fishing boat and followed him.

Then Jesus said to Andrew's brother, Simon, who is called Peter,

'You come, too.'

Further along the beach, there was a man mending his nets. His name was Zebedee. He had two sons, James and John. Jesus called them and they left their father and followed Jesus.

'From now on, I will make you fishers of men,' Jesus said.

'WE will get others to follow you, too. We will sing about you and then people will want to follow you,' called all the birds.

'I am sure you will. Thank you. We must all find ways to bring others to God.' Jesus smiled as he thanked the birds.

There was plenty of fun and the birds were happy down on the shore — tit-bits of fish, warm stones where they could bask in the sun and fresh air to fill their lungs.

Later on, Jesus said to the birds,

'I have chosen twelve Apostles, twelve leaders, to help me with my work.'

When the birds heard that, they called all their

friends together. The Wrens pushed their way to the front of the crowd, because they were responsible for spreading the news in all the land. When all the chirping and fluttering stopped, Jesus said,

'Here are the names. They are:

> (Simon) Peter
> Andrew,
> James,
> John,
> Philip,
> Bartholomew,
> Thomas,
> Matthew,
> James (son of Alphaeus),
> Lebbaeus (called Thaddaeus),
> Simon (the Cananaean),
> Judas (Iscariot).'

Jesus sent these men into all the places where the people were like lost sheep, sheep without a shepherd. They taught all the sad people about the wonderful things that Jesus did; how they, too, could do any number of things to make the world a better place.

'As Jesus says,' said Little Owl, 'if you can sing, sing for God. If you can dance, cook, build, farm, nurse, even if you sit and stare, do all these things for God and you will hear him say — thank you.'

Little Owl spoke with much wisdom and the other birds opened their beaks in amazement at what they heard. Little Owl looked a little amazed himself!

Jesus then told the birds to go with the Apostles wherever they went.

'Sing evensong with them every night,' he said.

'Oo, oo, he's chosen us, too, oo, oo!' Little Owl and all the other birds were so excited that they hardly knew which way to fly.

'Before you all go your different ways, I would say this to you,' said Jesus. 'Be not afraid. Keep my commandments. Love God, and love one another, helping all those in need. The Holy Spirit of God will be with you.'

Jesus rides into Jerusalem

Having worked among all the people for a while, the Apostles made their way back to Jerusalem so as to be in time for the Passover once again.

One by one, they met Jesus in a place called Bethphage on the Mount of Olives, near Bethany, which is on the road between Jericho and Jerusalem. Jesus said to two of them,

'Go into the village and you will find a donkey tied up. She will have her baby with her. Untie them and bring them to me. If anyone asks what you are doing, tell them that the Lord needs the donkey. You will have no trouble.'

The men did as Jesus asked and the villagers were happy to let the donkey and her baby go.

As soon as they reached where Jesus stood on the Mount of Olives, the men put their coats on the little donkey and Jesus climbed on to her back and rode down the hillside.

All the people followed; some even overtook Jesus. As they went, they cut down branches from the trees and threw them in the path of the donkey. People threw down their coats, too, and others waved big palm branches.

Some of the little birds became quite worried. They thought that there would be no branches left by night-time.

'Where shall we roost?' asked a flock of sparrows.

Barn Owl swooped down and said,

'Don't worry about roosts. Come and join in the singing. Listen to all those people!'

The sparrows decided to sing their own song as they flew in and out of the crowds.

> *'Jesus is our King.*
> *Join with us and sing*
> *Hymns of praise and psalms.*
> *Sing, blessed is our King.*
> *Sing "Hosanna," wave the palms.'*

The procession arrived at the gates of Jerusalem and all the people shouted,

'Blessed is he that cometh in the name of the Lord! Hosanna in the highest!'

Then the gates were flung wide and Jesus rode through in triumph.

It was a happy, happy time and the birds all found places where they could rest and watch. They found plenty of room in the nooks and crannies of the walls, too, where they could roost for the night.

Jesus dismounted and went into the Temple. He looked round and saw everything that was going on, but said nothing. He looked peaceful.

The next day was very different. Jesus, who had been so quiet and so gentle, went back into the Temple.

When he saw all the market stalls where people were selling cloth, pottery, chickens, goats and doves. He became very angry. He turned over the tables and the seats where the money-changers sat. He threw all the people out, turned round and asked,

'What do you mean by behaving like this in the Temple, my house?'

The people turned to look at the man, so gentle yesterday, so angry today. Then Jesus asked,

'Is it not written, my house shall be called a house

of prayer?' No one answered.

Jesus went on,

'But you have made it a den of thieves.'

Still no one spoke. As Jesus left the Temple, a dove cried, 'Vroo, croo, oo,' and lifted his head to Jesus, who stroked him as he passed.

The scribes and chief priests had heard Jesus in the Temple. They were amazed AND afraid, so they talked about how they could get rid of him.

Judas betrays Jesus

'Oh, oo, oo, oo, NOO,' cried Little Owl. 'Jesus has been in danger so often in his life. We must protect him.'

Nightingale flew to Little Owl's side and said,

'Jesus is a grown man now. All we can do is to be near him at all times. We must stay with him always, then he can ask us for help. We must watch and . . . .'

'And pray, too,' interrupted Little Owl.

While the two birds were talking, Barn Owl swooped down. He fluttered, over-balanced, toppled about and wiped his eyes with a wing. He could hardly speak, he was so upset.

'Barn Owl! What is the matter? Tell us,' said Nightingale, trying to soothe the poor bird with a gentle tune.

Barn Owl hissed and sniffed, then gurgled a little. He cleared his throat and said, between sobs,

'It's . . . one . . . of the . . . Apost . . . les, the one called . . .Judas.'

'What have you heard about Judas?' asked Little Owl.

Barn Owl tried hard to calm himself. Then he said,

'It's not only what I have heard, it is what I have seen, too. Judas went to the high priests; he whispered to them and they handed him silver money. As he was leaving, he called back to the priests — "the

one that I shall kiss, he will be the man to take."
Then all the high priests rubbed their hands and
smiled. What are we going to DO?'

Barn Owl hissed and sniffed again. Then Nightingale said,

'Surely, Judas has sold a friend, SOLD him.'

Barn Owl swayed on his long legs. He felt very ill,
thinking about Jesus being sold.

There was some chatting going on in a tree not far
from where the sad birds were. Then the two chat-
terers came to Barn Owl and said,

'Did we hear you mention silver? We are Magpies.
If you don't want your friend to keep his silver, we
will get it from him. We are collectors of things, you
know.'

'Yes, we do know that, but I don't know that Judas
is our friend any more. In any case, the silver is not
yours to take. That would be stealing. That is very
wrong. Be off with you! I don't know what things are
coming to. First a man sells his friend, then two
birds want to steal.' Barn Owl sighed and Nightingale called,

'Pioo, pioo, I feel I can sing only sadly. Listen to
my lament.'

Poor Nightingale! When she began to sing, no
sound would come. She cleared her throat and tried
again.

> *'Jesus my Lord has been sold,*
> *So, sadly, I sing with a sigh.*
> *Comfortless, I sit in the cold.*
> *Jealous men want him to die.*
> *A very sad story has yet to unfold*
> *But now, I'm too sad to sing or to fly.'*

Jesus and the Last Supper

Peter and John went to a house where, in the upper room, they put bread, wine, water and fruit on the table. Jesus joined all his Apostles there in the evening. Having his chosen ones with him and while they were eating, he said,

'One of you will betray me.'

They all asked,

'Is it I?'

During the meal, Jesus took bread. He blessed it, broke it and gave it to them, saying,

'This is my body.'

Of the wine, he said,

'This is my blood. Take it, all of you. Do this in remembrance of me.'

Judas left the room.

It was very quiet in that upper room. The birds had already left for their roosts. They knew that Jesus would be following them to the foot of the mountain range which was called Olivet.

As soon as supper was over, Jesus left, followed by his Apostles. He went to a place all by himself in the garden which was called Gethsemane. There, he prayed. A great stillness filled the garden. No trees moved at the foot of this mountain range. There was no sound except the whispering which came from Little Owl who looked around and said,

'Kiew, oo, I do believe we could hear a feather

drop.' Nightingale just nodded in answer. Suddenly, Little Owl let out a loud hoot, when he heard a crack.

'Someone in those bushes is up to no good,' he said.

This time, Nightingale flew to be near Little Owl. Everywhere felt dangerous. The two birds looked up and watched as little grey clouds passed softly over the sad face of Moon, wiping away her tears as they went. There was not a sound, now. The two, sitting together on a branch, could feel their hearts bumping. Little Owl swivelled his head round and round, keeping watch.

Suddenly, the silence was broken as, like a huge black cloud in the moonlit sky, all the birds flew in terror.

Little Owl and Nightingale nearly fell from the branch they were on as they watched the saddest sight. Men, rushing towards Jesus, shouted and the Apostles ran away. Then Judas, seeing Jesus, walked up to him and kissed him.

The men took Jesus and led him away. The garden looked sad. Moon hid behind the grey clouds and the stars shut their twinkling eyes.

Gradually, the birds returned to their roosts, but they did not sleep that night.

Jesus is crucified

It was very quiet in the early morning. There was no dawn chorus. The birds all gathered together and flew to the ramparts of the common hall where Jesus stood among a whole band of soldiers.

From the ramparts, some of the bigger birds tried to mob the soldiers in the hope that they would leave Jesus alone. But, sadly, they were killed, trying to save their friend. The birds who were left watched as the men stripped the clothes from Jesus and put on him a scarlet robe.

'Oo, oo, oo. Si, si, si. Chook, chook. Oo, ooo, oh,' they all cried, when they saw the men push a crown on to Jesus' head.

'I thought crowns were made of gold,' cried Blackbird.

'They are, usually,' said Magpie sadly, as he watched.

'But this one is made of long, very dangerous thorns! Look at the blood running down his face,' said a Fan-Tailed Dove. 'I am going to fly in and comfort Jesus. They are hurting him.'

Before any bird could warn the Dove, she had flown down to be with Jesus. He put out his hand and whispered,

'Thank you.' As he spoke, the little Dove was shot with an arrow by one of the cruel men.

Uable to watch any more, the birds flew to the

hillside, where they got a horrible shock. There, they found some men cutting down their favourite tree. This made them even more unhappy. From the bushes, the birds could see that the men carried with them hammer and nails.

When the tree was felled, the men cut it up and made a very heavy cross. This they carried down to the courtyard where Jesus stood.

The men took off the scarlet robe and made Jesus put on his own clothes again. This was very difficult for Jesus, who was in great pain and bleeding from his head. When he was ready, the men made poor Jesus carry that heavy cross all by himself, out of the courtyard, along the streets and up a long, winding, stony path, the crown of thorns hurting more with every step. He fell down several times, but was made to get up and stumble along the path. He was very sad and tired by now.

At the edge of the path, standing in the hot sun, was a very beautiful, tall, dark man from Africa. He was carrying a basket of eggs ready for market, when he met all the men pushing Jesus along. When Jesus fell again, this tall, handsome, strong man helped Jesus to his feet and said,

'I will carry your cross for you.'

He put down his basket of eggs and walked with the cross on his back. Jesus looked up at this kind man, who was called Simon, from Cyrene, but his mouth was too dry to speak any words. He tried to smile his thanks, but even that hurt his lips.

The time was nearly midday, when the sun was at its hottest. There was no shade on the way to the top of the green hill outside the city wall and Jesus had only a crown of thorns, no other cover for his head.

There on the hill, at midday, with the sun scorching the skin of Jesus, they nailed him to the cross.

Simon turned round and there, beside him, stood Mary. The Apostle John, whom Jesus loved, put his arm round Mary and tried to comfort her.

Simon left them and went away down the other side of the hill. He was so sad that he forgot all about his basket of eggs.

As the afternoon went on, the sky became very dark. Mary knelt at the foot of the cross, sobbing. It was very hard to watch her son dying such a terrible death. The wind blew and the rain began to lash down. Thunder rolled and lightning flashed.

Little Owl said to all the birds,

'You stay here while I go and bring Mary and John to the shelter of this cave.'

All the Blackbirds, Mistle Thrushes, Robins, Wrens, Song Thrushes, Pied Wagtails, Magpies, Sparrows, Barn Owls, other Little Owls, Turtle Doves, Nightingales, Starlings, Long-Tailed Tits, Woodpeckers, Cockerels, a whole flock of House

Martins and some Peacocks were sad and some of them didn't hear Little Owl. They could only think of their dearest friend hanging there in the storm, the dark, black storm, with rolling, angry skies.

Little Owl made his way through the storm. When he reached Mary and John, he took the edge of Mary's cloak in his beak and guided them both to the cave.

Not only had all the colour left the cheeks of Mary and John, but it had left all the birds, too. There seemed to be no colour any more in anything. The birds all looked grey and black, like the stormy sky outside.

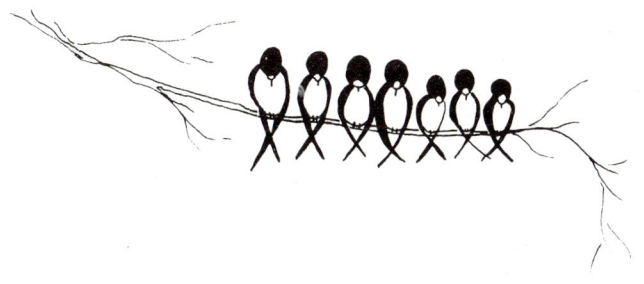

A flock of House Martins sat along a branch, looking just like a row of praying nuns. But their prayer wasn't silent. They hissed and whispered, then chatted and discussed how they could help Jesus. As they talked, there was a great, big crash. The cave shook. All the birds let out a cry and the earth trembled, making the birds think that it had split in two.

Soon, utterly exhausted, the birds fell asleep.

Jesus is laid to rest

Mary and John did not sleep. They crept out of the cave so as not to wake the birds. Soon they were in John's own home.

Not far away, there was a very rich man who had a beautiful garden. The man was Joseph of Arimathaea. He wrapped the body of Jesus in clean linen cloth and then took him to the garden.

In the garden, there was a brand new tomb which had been built in the rock. This is where Jesus was laid to rest.

Joseph and the men rolled a huge stone in front of the tomb so that no one could get anywhere near Jesus.

The next day, Saturday, was sad for everyone, because they all felt lost without Jesus.

The birds watched as people came to look at the tomb. Everywhere was quiet. Everything was without colour. The birds all looked pale. The sky was grey. The people had white faces.

The garden was beaten down by the storm and the trees still dripped rain, tears of sadness.

There was just one little bird with colour in his feathers. His wings and the end of his tail were black.

'Your red feathers are still wet! How did that happen? The rain stopped ages ago. Where have you been? What have you been doing? And look at your

beak! Come on, tell us what has been happening.'
All the birds fired questions at the little bird.

'Well, whatever my name WAS, it is now Crossbill.
I was with Mary and John at the foot of the cross
while Jesus hung there, dying. Mary cried bitterly
and I said that I would do my best to pull out the
nails from the hands and feet of Jesus, but it was no
use. My beak got twisted and now it is stuck. Then I
tried to pull out all those thorns crowning his head
and I got spluttered in blood. The thorns wouldn't
come out, either. I had to give up, so when I told
Mary, she stroked me and thanked me for trying,
saying,

> *"Trying to pull each nail*
> *From hands and feet, so pale,*
> *You worked with a will*
> *Even bending your bill,*
> *In remembrance*
> *We'll call you Crossbill."*

'Chook, chook,' called Blackbird. He was asking
Jenny Wren to tell Crossbill about the Last Supper
when Jesus broke bread, telling everyone to do just
that, in remembrance of him. 'Do this in remembrance of me,' Jesus had said.

'I will,' said Jenny Wren. 'I must spread that news
to all the birds who were not there. I'm sure Jesus
would not mind if we birds gave him a thought every
time we pick up a crumb of bread.'

'Hear, hear!' went up a chorus from all the birds
around. Then another bird arrived. She said nothing
for a moment, because she was so sad. Then she
looked up and whispered,

'I have been thinking. I never eat bread. I only
have insects, berries, spiders and earth-worms, but I
have. . . .' Nightingale stopped and stared in front of
her. Baby Earth-worm heard what she said as he

poked his head up through the grass below in the beautiful garden. As Nightingale made a dash for the worm, he shouted,

'Too late,' and he was gone. He'd slithered back into his hole.

'Never mind,' Nightingale said. 'I'll start again. I've been thinking. I want to remember this Holy Week. I am going to try to think of Jesus every time I have a meal. In fact, I shall sing this song.'

All the other birds thought that Nightingale had the right idea and they asked her to sing to them. She took a deep breath and opened her beak, but she didn't sing. She said,

'My song sounds as though it is only for bread-eaters, but that does not matter. It is for all of us at every meal-time. Are you ready?

> *'Every time that we break bread,*
> *Held in our feet or beak,*
> *We'll remember what he said,*
> *We'll remember Holy Week.*
> *When he said, "Take, all of you,*
> *My body is the bread,*
> *My blood, it is the wine.*
> *These holy things become the sign*
> *Of love for you, my love divine."*
> *Thank you, Lord, for what you give,*
> *In order that we all may live.'*

The risen Jesus is alive for ever

Very early the next morning, Sunday, still no birds sang. No breeze blew through the trees. The beautiful garden was very still. Little strips of mist, like baby fairy's swaddling bands, floated in the still air. Someone was smiling. The first smile for a whole week. That someone was Moon. She seemed to know something that no one else knew. There were no more tears to be wiped away by little grey clouds. They weren't grey any more. They were high in the sky, looking like happy, white woolly lambs. The sky they were in was as blue as Mary's cloak.

Little cradles and hammocks swung in the bushes and hedges. The dew-drops in the sunlight looked more like diamonds than moisture.

The sun sent out long, thin beams to warm the early morning air. As he rose into the sky, so Moon went down, still smiling.

All the flowers lifted up their heads and opened their petals. They, too, seemed to know a secret, like Moon.

'Vroo, croo, vroo, croo, where ARE you?' called a little white, Fan-Tailed Pigeon.

Robin heard the call and flew to Pigeon's side. 'Look! Look at the tomb! The stone has been rolled away! I've called and called Jesus, but there is no answer.' Pigeon spoke sadly and added,

'They must have taken him away. Who can we ask?'

Robin said,

'Quick, quick, quick. Let's ask Little Owl. He is so wise.'

'Oo, oo,' called Little Owl, hearing Robin's worried clicking call. Then, one by one, all the birds flew into the garden to hear the news that someone must have taken Jesus away. They were very sad.

'It is awful, not knowing what can have happened,' wailed a Turtle Dove. Many birds sang sad little songs. Then a bright little Blue Tit came flying in. She was very excited.

'Look! Look at each other! Look at our colours — they have all come back!' Glancing at the tomb, she said,

'Goodness gracious me! Where is Jesus? Who moved that great, huge stone? What's going on?'

'Oo, kiew, oo, let's ask that man over there. He seems to have put new life into all the flowers. He might know something. Most gardeners are very wise.'

'Not yet, not yet,' said Blackbird. 'Let's watch him for a while before we go too close.' The birds agreed.

Meanwhile, on the road to the city of Jerusalem, Simon, who had left his basket of eggs on the roadside, while he carried the cross for Jesus, was amazed when he saw the eggs. There they were, still in their basket, but they had changed. They were all brightly coloured. Simon picked up the basket and when he reached the city, he hid the eggs in all sorts of places. Then, he called all the children together and told them what had happened.

'Now you have heard my story, go egg-hunting! They are all yours.' What a lovely Easter Egg hunt they all had!

Back in the garden, the birds made up their minds to go and ask the gardener where the body of Jesus had been taken. They hopped close, then jumped back. They flew into a tree close by, then jumped on to the ground. The man was so quiet and smiled at the birds. He kept very still so as not to frighten them.

Robin was very bold and went right up to the man, who put out both hands and said, as he looked up to all the other birds, too,

'I am sorry, I have no crumbs, no bread with me.' When the birds saw the prints of the nails in those hands, they knew it was Jesus and not the gardener.

The dawn chorus burst into song.

> *'Our Lord is risen indeed.*
> *With happy news, we'll feed*
> *The children everywhere,*
> *Our joy, we long to share.'*

After much singing, Jenny Wren flew away to tell the good news to everyone. In fact, many Wrens flew throughout the land.

'He died to save us ALL,' sang the little Wrens, holding their periscopes high in the air.

'Go on, little birds, go and teach them all.' Jesus waved as the birds left to spread the news.

Mary, with John, saw all the birds overhead. She knew that Jesus was alive and said to John, as they watched,

'HE made their glowing colours.'